How To Make $5,500 Per Month Writing E-Books

Tim Jastens

ISBN: **1497494974**
ISBN-13: **978-1497494978**

DEDICATION

This book is dedicated to first time authors who are trying to get their manuscripts published. Follow these guidelines and you can begin making $5,500 per month from writing E-books too.

ACKNOWLEDGMENTS

To all of my friends in the business world who taught me the ins and outs of the publishing industry. I thank you for your knowledge and guidance.

INTRODUCTION TO E-BOOKS

In a world where printed books are becoming a thing of the past writers have had to get creative at how they share their works with the rest of the universe.

E-Books have become a new trend around the world. Not only can you download E-books to read on your desktop or laptop computer, but now you can download apps that will allow you to download and read E-books directly from your smart phone.

With so many different E-reading programs available for

download now it makes sense that printed books are quickly become a thing of the past. E-books account for more than half of all book sales now days.

Of course, there are still plenty of traditional readers out there who grew up reading printed books that will always want to hold a physical book in their hand where they can turn the pages, but a new generation of readers who only know books in the form of E-books are quickly growing up and becoming adults.

This book is being printed as a printed book that you are reading simply to reach the generation of people left who grew up on printed books and want to hold this physical book in their hands.

Twenty years from now this book would not even be printed as a book.

We live in a society that even puts our children's textbooks for school on an Ipad so they can download and pull up the class textbook at any time no matter where the students are at. We have all but eliminated the need for children to carry big book bags full of 5 or 6 different textbooks for all of the different classes they are taking.

You can like it or not like it but reality is the printed book will soon be a thing of the past. E-books are the now and the future. As a writer, you must learn to adapt to the changing environment of your business.

Writers are constantly faced with the question of "How can I communicate my message or information to the most amount of people in the quickest amount of time in the most cost efficient way?" E-books are a great answer to this question.

Throughout this book we will be covering several positive aspects to E-book writing. While we will also examine some of the disadvantages to E-books versus the traditional paperback book, we will see that there are very few disadvantages compared to the amount of positive advantages offered by E-books.

The advantages are numerous both for you as a writer and more importantly for the readers (your audience) in which you are trying to communicate with. Some key points that will be covered in this book include;

-Traditional Publishing versus Self-Publishing

Before we can even begin the discussion of E-books versus Paperback books we first must understand the relationship between a traditional publisher and a self-publisher.

Traditional Publishing houses have been around for centuries. There are so many amazing books that come from traditional publishing houses. The concept behind a traditional publisher is that the author of the manuscript being published never has to pay a fee for production of their manuscript. In some cases the author may even receive a healthy royalty advancement because the publishing houses believes that the book will sell well.

In order to have your manuscript selected by a traditional publishing house for publication you first need to have a concept or idea of your story. You do not need a completed draft to submit a manuscript proposal by any means but you will need a very detailed outline of your manuscript along with a chapter by chapter description of every chapter. In most cases publishers will ask you to submit two or three completed chapters of your manuscript so that they can review it.

Should a traditional publisher like your concept and idea they may choose to offer you a publishing contract and offer you a royalty advancement. Royalty advancements can vary in their size but I have seen anywhere from $2500.00-$300,000.00. In some cases it may be a higher advancement than that.

Upon offering you a royalty advancement the publisher will give you a few months to finish up the manuscript before you submit it to them for editing. The advancement is meant to help compensate you for the time you will need to spend focusing on really cleaning up the book and making it flow. Basically, if you are offered a contract with an advancement you should already know you have a great manuscript. The next step for you is cleaning it up and making it shine. You are going to want to have it polished up for the millions of eyes that are going to be reading your book.

The advantage to traditional publishing is that they provide you with editorial services and marketing services free of charge to you. Essentially what is happening is the publishing house is buying your manuscript from you. Now that the traditional publisher has ownership in your manuscript they definitely have interest in making sure all of the editing and marketing services are professionally done and well executed. Now that both you and the traditional publisher are on the same team and both have ownership of your manuscript you will be working with them on both editing and marketing. The big advantage I like about traditional publishers is that they have interest in how the book sells. They make money from your book sales as they will keep a percentage of sales from all of your royalty payments.

Unlike in self-publishing where the publisher has no ownership of your manuscript and likely has little to no interest on how many copies of your book are sold during the lifetime of your book.

The traditional publisher will provide you with your own publicist and marketing representative that will assist you in lining up book signings and speaking engagements. For those of you writers who are writing about a niche subject like Health or Money or Psychology you have what is known as a niche market.

Meaning, the content that you are publishing already has an audience with many interested parties wanting to read about the information you are providing them. Niche markets are awesome for book sales. It is highly likely that you will obtain professional speaking engagements that will allow you to take your own books and sell them at conferences to your fans and colleagues.

These in person/direct sales opportunities are the greatest sales opportunity that you will have for your book. If you have a niche subject you are writing about you already have an advantage of the author who does not have a niche subject or is writing a fantasy novel. Niche subjects will always sell themselves. The more work you put into marketing and advertising your book the more sales you will earn.

It is for those writers who do not write about niche subjects that traditional publishing houses come in handy for. The traditional publisher is a mass marketing machine and can help you turn your story into a niche subject in the world if it was not already before.

Traditional Publishers are great for those seasoned writers who have a lot of experience writing and can produce a 100,000 word novel fairly quickly. Traditional Publishers are not idea for first time authors and I find that most authors who are signed by traditional publishing houses began their writing careers by self-publishing.

The big disadvantage to traditional publishing is that when sharing ownership of your manuscript you are also sharing all of the profits your book earns with the traditional publisher.

What does this mean for you? You will earn a much lesser percentage of book royalty sales from the traditional publishing route than you will from self-publishing. Add this with the idea that traditional publishers spend a lot of money marketing the books that they do publish and put a lot of time into the books that they hope will become best sellers which means they will likely only publish 10-20 manuscripts per year.

Imagine having your first manuscript sitting in a traditional publisher's office awaiting review. Your manuscript is sitting in an office along with 30,000 other manuscripts that have been submitted throughout the year. They may pick 20 out of 30,000. The odds of a first time author being chosen for publication by a traditional publisher are not in your favor.

They may have several submissions already planned out for the year that are from their current authors. In my experience in the publishing industry the traditional publisher's current authors who have had success with book sales will always receive first priority for a publishing contract over the first time author with no proven sales history. It can be difficult to obtain a publishing contract from a traditional publishing house. In the past, authors would just sit around in frustration receiving rejection letter after rejection letter from publishing houses. Thanks to the invention of the concept of self-publishing authors no longer need to sit around and wait on acceptance letters from traditional publishing houses. In fact, authors now have more control and power over the traditional publishing houses than they have ever had before.

Self-Publishing is a fairly new concept that has not been around for too long. When self-publishing a manuscript you retain all rights to your work and are the sole owner of your manuscript. You hold all copyrights and your manuscript cannot be copied or reproduced by anyone without your written permission and consent.

Self-Publishing offers authors a new and unique way to publish their manuscript and information that never existed before. It gives the author complete ownership and control of their own manuscript and allows the author to control his or her own destiny. If you still desire to be published by a traditional publishing house self-publishing can actually help you increase your chances of landing a big contract from a publishing house. There are many examples of best-selling books on the market today that were self-published before the author was offered a publishing contract because their self-published book had a tremendous amount of success.

A recent example of a self-published book that caught the attention of a traditional publishing house is the <u>50 Shades of Grey</u> series by author E.L. James.

This trilogy took the world by storm when James wrote about her sexual fantasies and desires in the bedroom for bondage and fetish play. She has racked in over $85 Million dollars already for her thrilling adventurous book.

Here is an example of someone who probably submitted proposal after proposal to publishing houses around the world only to be sent rejection letter after rejection letter in the mail. Why?

Because she was a first time author and the writing was not the greatest. Fortunately what helped her sell her book as a self-published book is the content of the book and the subject matter. I have talked to many people about the <u>50 Shades of Grey</u> book series who were not so much impressed by the writing of the book but admitted they only bought the book because of all of the hype it was getting about sex.

Here is another prime example of an author who took advantage of a niche market to sell massive amounts of copies of her manuscript.

Once the author achieved some success at the self-publishing level and the book was getting a lot of attention the traditional publishing houses wanted to get their name on the book and gain ownership in her manuscript so that they could earn money from it as well. It is all about creating interest in your manuscript. If you can create some interest on your own without the help of a traditional publisher the chances are a traditional publisher will notice your manuscript and want to be a part of it.

While some authors might have the goal of landing that contract with a traditional publishing house one day, I encourage authors to let go of that dream or idea and explore the world of self-publishing and all of the tremendously positive advantages self-publishing has to offer. As mentioned earlier, self-publishing gives the author ownership of his or her own manuscript. This allows the author to make any edits to the manuscript at any point and time throughout the life of the book without seeking permission from the traditional publishing house.

With the elimination of co-ownership in your manuscript, self-publishing offers the author a much higher royalty percentage. An author might expect to earn fifteen percent of their books profits from a traditional publisher throughout the life of the book along with that generous royalty advancement that they received. In self-publishing an author will not receive a generous royalty advancement but will instead earn anywhere from sixty to eighty percent of their books royalty sales throughout the lifetime of their manuscript. The potential for profit is much greater long term than it is with a traditional publishing house.

While traditional publishing might offer an author a huge sum of money in the short term in a royalty advancement the author is trapped in contract for life of the book and only able to receive around fifteen percent of their profits from the book as the publisher will keep the majority of the profits for themselves.

A self-published author will be on their own for marketing purposes. A self-publishing company will mainly provide formatting services for your book. Meaning, they will prepare your book for production as a paperback book and an E-book. In some cases you will have the option to have a hardback book created as a special edition but please note that the cost of printing a hard cover book is significantly higher than the cost of printing a paperback book.

In self-publishing the author will submit an edited manuscript that the self-publisher will format into a book as an E-book and a paperback book. Many self-publishers also offer editing services however they are fairly pricey.

It is my preference to hire someone I know to do some editing for me before I submit a manuscript for publication with any self-publishing company. The turnaround time for the release of your manuscript from the time you email it to the self-publisher is much faster than it is with traditional publishing.

In traditional publishing sometimes their book production

schedule is planned out for an entire year or two. This means that as an author you might be offered a book contract and then sit and wait for two years before your book even begins production. Self-publishers will begin production on your book as soon as they have your manuscript's file and payment for production of your manuscript.

Self-Publishing fees can be fairly pricey. I recommend doing some research to find a company that is going to give you the best quality of manuscript for the best price. I would not ever pay a company thousands upon thousands of dollars to produce a manuscript. It simply should not cost that much. If you have to pay more than a few hundred dollars for the formatting and production of your manuscript with a self-publishing company I recommend steering away from them and continuing your search.

Another added advantage to self-publishing is that many self-publishers offer print on demand services. As a self-published author you will have to buy copies of your book at a discounted rate before you can begin selling them to friends and family or at conferences you attend and speak at. The price you pay for printing depends upon the publisher but CreateSpace offers a very affordable printing program and it is entirely print on demand. Print on demand is a huge gift to first time authors. With many publishing houses the only way you are able to obtain copies of your own book is to buy a required number of books that could be 50-100 at a time. Usually a lot of publishing houses have a minimum amount of books you can order. With print on demand if I just wanted to order one copy per week I could. That is the best feature I like about self-publishing.

This concludes book I which was an introduction to learning about different publishing options you have with publishing your manuscript. Now we are ready to move onto diving into the concept of E-books and how they compare and contrast to paperback books. Read <u>How To Make $5,500 Per Month Writing E-books Book II</u> next. Book II will be released in the spring of 2014.

ABOUT THE AUTHOR

Tim Jastens resides in Thousand Oaks, California with his wife Pam and daughter Susan. Tim is an entrapranuer and businessman who has been in the publishing industry for years.

Tim Jastens